When You Love a Dog

Written by M.H. Clark   Illustrated by Tatsuro Kiuchi

When you love a dog, someone waits for you,

with a true and joyful heart.

And everything is as it should be,

just as soon as you walk through the door—

it's time for ear scratches, and belly rubs,

and rolling around on the floor.

When you love a dog,

the world is full of wonder—

every walk and every morning,

every single night.

And the warm eyes looking up at you

are full of love and light.

You have a friend through all of it,

who's up for anything—

who looks forward, who can hardly wait,

who wants what the world will bring.

And that world is
all *today*, *today*,
and *you*, and *you*,
and *you*!

And this moment, right here, is a perfect one.

It's one to hold on to.

And there's silliness and sincerity

and trouble and play—

sometimes all together,

in the very same day.

When you love a dog, you're loved in return

for everything you are.

And the simplest things are the very best things—

a head in your lap, a treat in your hand,

a ride to the park in the car.

And it's a comfort, on the hard days, to come home to this—

this endless bright being, this big sloppy kiss.

When you love a dog, you are understood.

You are seen and you are heard,

without ever needing to ask.

Without even saying a word.

What's shared here is for always—

a lifetime of moments and beautiful days.

When you love a dog, someone waits for you—

you're the one they want to see.

What a gift it is to come home to this,

this love is here for me.

COMPENDIUM®

live inspired

Written by: M.H. Clark

Illustrated by: Tatsuro Kiuchi

Art Directed by: Megan Gandt Guansing

Edited by: Kristin Eade

Library of Congress Control Number: 2017958299 | ISBN: 978-1-943200-98-6

6th printing. Printed in China with soy inks on FSC®-Mix certified paper.

Create meaningful moments with gifts that inspire.

CONNECT WITH US

live-inspired.com | sayhello@compendiuminc.com

@compendiumliveinspired
#compendiumliveinspired